Weimaramers
Show Off

Sabrina Lakes

Sporting Dogs
FETCH MASTERS
Show Off

xist Publishing

Check out all of the books in the Fetch Masters Series

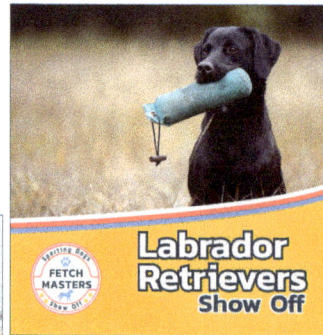

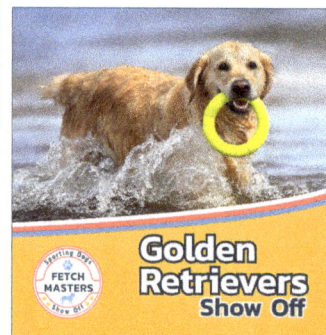

Cocker Spaniels Show Off

Weimaraners Show Off

Labrador Retrievers Show Off

Golden Retrievers Show Off

Published in the United States by Xist Publishing
www.xistpublishing.com
© 2025 Copyright Xist Publishing

First Edition
Hardcover ISBN: 978-1-5324-5531-5
Paperback ISBN: 978-1-5324-5532-2
eISBN: 978-1-5324-5530-8

PUBLISHED IN TEXAS

Table of Contents

Introduction to Weimaraners

Weimaraners are medium to large-sized dogs known for their sleek, silver-gray coats and strong, athletic builds. Originally from Germany, they were bred to assist hunters in tracking and retrieving game. Weimaraners are friendly, energetic, and intelligent dogs who love to run and explore. They are often called the "gray ghosts" because of their coat color and how they move quietly through the fields.

Fun Facts About Weimaraners

Weimaraners are incredibly fast runners, able to cover long distances quickly. They have a sharp sense of smell, which makes them great at tracking animals. Weimaraners are known for their loyalty and love to be with their families. Their sleek coats don't require much grooming, and they are often admired for their elegant appearance. Weimaraners have a lot of energy and need plenty of exercise every day.

What is Sporting?

Sporting means helping hunters find and bring back animals like birds and deer. Weimaraners are skilled at tracking because of their sharp noses and excellent running speed. They are also good at retrieving, carefully carrying the game back to the hunter. Sporting dogs like Weimaraners need a lot of energy and love to be outdoors.

Why Weimaraners are Great Sporting Dogs

Weimaraners are great sporting dogs because they are strong, fast, and have a sharp sense of smell. They can run quickly through open fields and track animals across long distances. Weimaraners are also gentle with the animals they retrieve, using their soft mouths to carry game without damaging it. Their intelligence and energy make them perfect for many types of sporting activities.

Training a Weimaraner

Training a Weimaraner can be fun and rewarding. Start with simple commands like "sit," "stay," and "come." Use treats and praise to reward good behavior. Weimaraners love learning new things and respond well to positive training. Keep training sessions short and interesting. Practice regularly to help your Weimaraner stay focused and happy.

Games to Help Weimaraners Learn

Games are a great way to train Weimaraners. Play fetch to teach them to bring things back. Hide treats around the yard or house to help them use their noses to find things. You can also play "hide and seek" with their favorite toy. These games help Weimaraners stay active and enjoy learning.

A Day in the Life of a Sporting Weimaraner

Weimaraners start their day with lots of energy. After a good breakfast, they are ready to head out to the fields. They run quickly through tall grass and open spaces, using their sharp noses to track game. Weimaraners are excited to be part of the hunt and are always ready for action.

Working with the Team

Weimaraners work closely with hunters and other dogs. When they find an animal, they use their speed to follow it and alert the hunter. Weimaraners are gentle with the game they retrieve, carrying it carefully in their mouths. They love being part of the team and enjoy the challenges of working outdoors.

Caring for a Weimaraner

Weimaraners need healthy meals to keep up their energy. They usually eat twice a day. Their short, sleek coats don't need much grooming, but brushing their fur helps keep it clean and shiny. Regular grooming also helps you check for ticks and other pests. Make sure to trim their nails regularly to keep them comfortable.

Keeping Your Weimaraner Healthy

Exercise is very important for Weimaraners. They love to run, play, and explore every day. Regular walks, playtime, and games help them stay happy and healthy. Weimaraners also need regular check-ups with the vet to ensure they stay in good health. They thrive when they have plenty of exercise and time with their family.

Weimaraners at Rest

After a busy day, Weimaraners need time to rest. They enjoy napping in cozy places and love being near their families. Rest helps them recharge for the next day's adventures. Weimaraners are happiest when they are with their loved ones, even if they are just relaxing.

Fun Activities for Weimaraners

Weimaraners love to play even when they are resting. They enjoy toys that squeak, bounce, or move quickly. Puzzle toys are great for keeping their minds active, and they love spending time with their family. Weimaraners are loyal and playful dogs who always enjoy time with their loved ones.

Glossary

Commands   Words or signals used to tell a dog what to do, like "sit" or "stay."

Coat   The fur covering a dog's body, which can be short or long.

Ears   The part of the dog's head used for hearing and helping with scent detection.

Exercise   Physical activity like running or playing that keeps dogs healthy and happy.

Grooming   Caring for a dog's coat, ears, and nails to keep them clean and healthy.

Hunter   A person who uses dogs like Weimaraners to help find and retrieve game.

Nose   The part of a dog's face used for smelling and tracking scents.

Retrieve   Bringing something back, such as a bird, to a hunter.

Vet   A doctor who takes care of animals and helps keep them healthy.

Index

Keyword List

Nouns	Verbs	Adjectives	Adverbs
animal	alert	active	actively
breakfast	bring	athletic	eagerly
coat	carry	curious	easily
command	eat	fast	fast
dog	explore	focused	gently
ears	find	friendly	happily
energy	follow	gentle	quickly
exercise	groom	gray	sharply
family	help	happy	skillfully
field	hide	healthy	well
game	learn	intelligent	
grass	play	loyal	
hunter	praise	quick	
nose	retrieve	sharp	
speed	run	short	
team	search	sleek	
toy	sit	smart	
treat	sniff	strong	
vet	track	tall	
Weimaraner	work	trained	

Sporting Dogs

FETCH
MASTERS

Show Off

www.ingramcontent.com/pod-product-compliance
Lightning Source LLC
LaVergne TN
LVHW070835080426
835508LV00031B/3474